Corrigenda for Costafine Town

First published in 2021 by Blue Diode Press
30 Lochend Road
Leith
Edinburgh EH6 8BS
www.bluediode.co.uk

ISBN: 978-1-9164051-9-6

Typesetting: Rob A. Mackenzie.
text in Pilgrim LT Roman

Cover art: Louisa Hodgson, 'The Collingwood Monument, Tynemouth, Trafalgar Night, c.1930–38 (tempera on panel)' © *Tyne & Wear Archives & Museums / Bridgeman Images*

Cover design and typography: Rob A. Mackenzie

Diode logo design: Sam and Ian Alexander.

Printed and bound by Imprint Digital, Exeter, UK.
https://digital.imprint.co.uk

Corrigenda for Costafine Town

Jake Morris-Campbell

Blue Diode Press
Edinburgh

For Kate, Gruffydd
and the Morris-Campbell-Flannery clan

Caer Urfa

Notes and Acknowledgements

I owe heartfelt thanks to the editors of the following publications in which some of these poems first appeared: Bare Fiction, Fragmented Voices, Land of Three Rivers: the Poetry of North-East England (Bloodaxe Books), New Boots and Pantisocracies, Newcastle Evening Chronicle/ The Journal, Poetry Salzburg Review, Stand, Under the Radar (Nine Arches Press), Volume and Wild Court.

These poems were written with the support of a Northern Bridge studentship. Grateful acknowledgement is therefore made to the Arts and Humanities Research Council (UK) and to friends, peers and colleagues at Newcastle University, not least: Bill Herbert, Alex Niven, Tara Bergin, Jacob Polley, Sean O'Brien and Sinéad Morrissey. Thanks, too, to Paul Batchelor at Durham University, and to the Queen's lot in Belfast.

Big thanks to Rory Waterman for providing spirited suggestions for improvement. I also need to thank Ian Seed at the University of Chester for offering guidance, while former colleagues and friends along the banks of the Dee provided the very first sparks that would form the tinder for these poems. R.I.P. Derek Alsop.

Special thanks are owed to John Challis, who offered generous feedback on early drafts of many of these poems. There's one in the pumps at the Bridge Hotel for you, marra. Other early readers who helped me see what I was doing with this book, and are deserving of credit, are: Rishi Dastidar, Suzannah V. Evans, Bernadette McAloon and Robert Selby.

Several of these poems enjoyed early run-outs in multimedia formats. The Bede poems were written for and exhibited alongside artworks as part of the Heritage Lottery Funded initiative, 'Stringing Bedes: A Poetry and Print Pilgrimage' in 2015–16 at venues in Sunderland and South Tyneside. Thank you to Keith Bowey and my fellow walkers. 'Errata Slip for a Northern Town' and 'Akenside Syndrome' were first broadcast on the Rich Seams podcast, curated by Andrew McMillan and commissioned by the Durham Book Festival in 2018. 'Pons Aelius City Limits' was written for the interactive app-based walking tour, 'Steps in Time', commissioned for the 2017 Newcastle Poetry Festival, while 'Each Pebble its Part' was written for the 2016 Newcastle Poetry Festival as part of the 'Northern Landscapes: Picture Poems' exhibition at the Ex Libris Gallery. Adapted lines are from Basil Bunting's Briggflatts.

Mike Collier commissioned 'Dawn Chorus: Cleadon Village' for his 2017 exhibition 'Singing the World' at Cheeseburn Grange Sculpture Park, Northumberland. This poem also features in Mike Collier ed., 'Songs of Place and Time: Birdsong and the Dawn Chorus in Natural History and the Arts' (Art Editions North/ Bath Spa University, 2021). Mike has been a long-time champion of my work and his encouragement is appreciated.

Three of these poems were translated into Czech by Natalie Nera as part of the Cadena Magica project.

I road-tested many of these poems at various open-mic nights, conferences and other reading series around the country and abroad prior to setting them down in print. If you had me on, thanks so much.

Contents

Costafine town, it's a fine town, I'm coming home
I feel so lonely, I've been too long away.
Costafine Town, it's a fine town, I'm coming home.
I wish I'd never made up my mind to stray.

– Splinter, 'Costafine Town', *The Place I Love* (Dark Horse Records, 1974)

A184 Hymn

For Peter Armstrong, William Martin and the Lads. FTM.

Gods of the Felling bypass
Gods of Whitemare Pool

Converse at the castra
reveal Wrekendyke

Let all the lights
at Heworth and Wardley
turn amber to green

For the sake
of the desolate North
for the sake
of distrustful experts
let Testo's big-wheel sink

Chase flea circus freaks
down Cut Throat Dene

No flint knap
no sword clash
no horse punch
no human cannonball

Whoever watches over
lads in their twenties
whoever's faith goes beyond
döner meat and chips

cap the meter at twenty
and let us care nothing
for the battle of Boldon Hill

An Imposter Alights at Horsley Hill

Riding the same loop
round the town you were born in
trying every stop til one welcomed
you as wanderer returned.

Round the town you were born in
as at Keppel Street bus station
you wait as wanderer returned,
clouds buffering on far horizons.

At Keppel Street bus station
waiting to be demolished
clouds buffer on far horizons
as some master plan to be revealed.

Waiting to be demolished
you once knew where each stand went
as some master plan to be revealed
and you held the blueprints.

You once knew where each stand went
but rode the same loop
like it held the blueprints
trying every stop til one welcomed.

White Mare of Marsden

For Gruffydd

Fret, fret, fret, these days of diluted air,
we take to Quarry Lane searching for the mare:
me and me son, walking off the stupor
in an arcane pilgrimage to the edge of the edge
of town, where as a bairn I was often taken
and told the same stories my great-grandfather
handed down: when the road out
was seldom galloped, tales unassailable,
narratives lapped up as broth on buttered stotties.
Now, the tips of her ears, dainty white fronds,
protrude above bushes I was never taught the names for
but her flank is invisible – covered by what I'll call
a *thicket* of green, blooming and puffing out
its nectar on the first spring-like day of the year.
Brine blowing up from the bay swells
with three or four birds' choruses known
from years of hearing the same shrill on repeat.
Meanwhile the treadmill sea does the rote work
of any inferior maritime metaphor as the stone harp
at Tynemouth (an image borrowed from another poet)
fills gaps in post-war cottages on streets called
Cragside and The Lonnen, adding to the collage
I'll call a *communal fresco* – this Trompe-l'œil
that I'm formulating for self and son –
all self-same sons who'll make their way back
up these little screes to find the image overgrown,
no local authority or Trust-erected panel in sight,
but a knowing, sinew-deep, that the story's just right.

The Village that Vanished

All the bitter day waves smash into Smugglers' Cove and
  Byer's Hole.
The sky has failed to lift and a shipwright's hoolie blows doon
  King Street.
Sometime soon we'll re-pack the van, lock the door, gan from
  here.
Away from foghorn bass and herring-gull staccato we'll wake
to brighter light, wind in tune. There'll be no need to tell the
  bairns
about Jobling or Fairles, riots at Mill Dam, the death of
  Palmer's Yard,
except to say they all kindled in a town where no town
  should be,
where for years the houses inched closer to the cliffs, buddleia
  crept
into lintels and sycophants threw gasoline onto the pyre.

Fret

Tell all your banshees I don't work the land
and am glad of it. No father and son team
tilling the field, scything barley by hand,
unbroken patterns in the rigg and furrow.

Everything apocryphal will have to go
if we're to compete on the global stage.
The parish no longer bakes its own bread;
district water works are defunct.

I never saw the white mare of Marsden
whinnying by the old quarry, the rag 'n' bone
man calling through fret. But I saw two
vestigial towers, industrious on the skyline –

knew the bucolic fable flooding the echo-chamber.

Akenside Syndrome

'…in general, cliverness also meant softiness, hard Geordie
meant hard lad, lack of accent meant softy. Geordie, a
badge of hardness, taalkin' posh or properly or English
meant collaborator, sneak, crawler, softy.' —David John
Douglass, *Geordies – Wa Mental, Wa Off Wa Fuckin Heeds!*

My voice choosing whether it knaas or knows
while lost on campus looking for the hall.
Geordie syllables caught in me throat.

Repairman with faded anchor and swallow
tattoos speaks a language my Granda bawls
while aa wonder what it is aa knaa I know.

Puzzled, I ponder which way to gan or go
while he points: forst on ya left, nee bother at aall.
Geordie syllables free in his throat.

Cleaners and canteen staff in the shadow
of the academy don't need to call
Geordie syllables caught in their throats.

From the Robinson Library I can see Gallow-
gate: thousands of accents that are Hebburn, Walls-
end, while my tongue stumbles: knaa or know?

Considering where my voice is at home:
how a Tyneside accent can make iz galled;
torn over when it's right to knaa or know.
Geordie syllables caught in my throat.

Errata Slip for a Northern Town

'The choices open to women and men today – even amongst the underprivileged—may be more numerous than in the past, but what has been lost irretrievably is the choice of saying: this is the centre of the world.' —John Berger, *and our faces, my heart, brief as photos*

For:	*Read:*
'The Metro in a hurry to pass the sunken gasometer.'	'The end of the line is also its beginning.'
'Crumbling asbestos of failed industrial units.'	'Glow of fireweed against rusted railing.'
'Identikit new houses no-one round here can afford.'	'It's the people that make the place.'
'Midday drinkers outside Annie McCarthy's.'	'Hazy summer evenings at the Shields Riviera.'
'Seagulls screaming down Keppel Street.'	'Melody of seabirds strumming the shore.'
'The congestion and overpriced car parks.'	'The end of the oil age is soon upon us.'
'Tombstone suicides at Marsden Bay.'	'She lived a long life soothed by the sea.'
'A dead-end high street with no decent shops.'	'A thriving local economy of independent retailers.'

'An absolute lack
of intellectual curiosity.'

'A barren peninsula
of backward-looking bigots.'

'Those who had to leave
and those who burn to.'

'The streets are named
after long-dead poets.'

'A stunning seaside town
open to the world.'

'You could spend your life here;
you could be happy.'

Operation Square Leg

For Michael Mulvihill

'Are we living in a land | Where sex and
horror are the new Gods?' – Frankie Goes to
Hollywood, *Two Tribes*

Some place in Soviet Russia, a Commander
sets down his lunch-break tea,
selects the next slide on his inventory:
Port of Tyne, South Shields.

With a cartographer's grace, he plots
a diagrammatic map of strategic targets:
munitions lines at Scotswood,
steelworks in Consett, the slake at Jarra.

Higher up the command chain,
over salvers of mackerel and stuffed olives,
Generals signal the go-ahead
and a domino of procedures fall.

My parents are disco-dancing in Rupert's
nightclub: my mother making plans
in my father's spindly hands,
a kaleidoscope of grace.

Glinting in their eyes is the flash
tearing the skies
the intercontinental ballistic missile
makes in the seconds before impact.

Have You Heard the One About the Lions?

It's 1985 and an Ashington ex-miner
is goading my Granda, who's fitting out a bookies
in the centre of Nottingham, saying the lions
on the Council House steps only roar
when a virgin walks past.

It's 2015 and I'm trembling on Jäger-bombs
on a tram to Hucknall telling Ali's mate,
a builder with blond cheeks and sandpaper hands,
that by voting for the Tories
he's shot himself and his littl'un in the foot.

In the version of the joke I re-tell
to keep conversation flowing and give the impression
that I'm one of the lads, Ali is the virgin,
his mate is my Granda fitting out the bookies
and I'm the ex-miner from Ashington.

In the typescript of the anecdote I edit
all the lads have gone and the lions refuse to roar.

Superlative

Here's me theory: every hand car wash boasting the slogan
BEST IN TOWN on gaudy billboards written in geet big fonts

is the quiet envy of every languishing poet with an inferiority
    complex
wishing to craft their lyrics with considered sincerity.

I have thought of so many ways to document this place
which all swivel back round to bad imitations of Philip Levine.

Ghosts of the Jarra marchers are always trying to pierce these
    poems.
Nar: it isn't five-to-five at three and a half Dock Street.

No tools are being downed and the pumps at the Holborn
Rose & Crown are condemned to brownfield and future
    development.

Can I say: Let the cash registers keep on chugging; let every bairn
get their fill of mutten when the labour this narrative was forged

upon rests unbidden on the shoulders of Eastern European
    workers
and their chilblains? These are the bodies my fellow denizens

supposedly deplore: young lads pulling rags through mangles,
polishing the bonnets of imported Audis.

I say in my head but not out loud that this kind of graft
is totally pure knowing I'll never have to do it myself.

I say in my Twitter stream but not in my ballot that I deplore
my contingent contract at the Russell Group institution

a few miles up the river, but you need to know that I scabbed
    today
or felt like a scab for not joining the union in the first place.

Now our overloads can cut with shears not scissors,
this should be a praise-poem for all precariously employed

scorched earth workers facing obsolescence, but who am I
to speculate on the business model employed on this old
    forecourt

when I'm surrounded by bubbles? So I'll send down the window,
exchange a slippery fiver for a cherry air-freshener, dangle it

on its elastic from the rear-view and try not to solemnise
cathedrals of scrap metal as the saccharine aroma starts to
    flower.

Before letting go of the destructive notion of a mid-twentieth century working-class hero narrating my quarter-life crisis, indulge me to speculate how

he'd describe in jubilant detail a scene in which three generations of Campbells walked down Langholm Road: my grandfather leading the pack, a dozen Carlings in; my Dad next, hair not yet thin; me at the back—expectant protégée. These men, he'd say, knew the difference between crankshafts and flywheels. Wor lad has a decent understanding of stress--ed and unstressed syllables, some synonyms for work but no original definition. He'd recount how, even now, I was chewing over a half-decent but ultimately forgettable simile comparing how graft hung heavy on men like them to the way cold clings to a person entering a warm house from a wintry storm. Just on cue the barriers would go down. A diesel engine heaving from Sunderland would be said to throw the fireweed back against the sleepers like birds' hair in Pantenne adverts [!] but the metaphor would jar, de-railing the action to end abruptly on a close-up of flashing warning lights, the distant [clack/roar/chug] of another train coming further down the track
                              three figures frozen in silhouette

        while the eyes of his great-gran, gran and mam roll
    across the centuries

Restoration

Eva has come from Košice, Slovakia
to Quarry Lane, South Shields
to restore matchbox-by-matchbox
a fresco of Marsden Rock.

Charlie is telling us this over pints
of John Smith's as we wait for topside
of beef, Yorkies and spuds.
Newcastle go a goal down

to whichever London team
but our focus is the fireplace
above which three-quarters
of her handiwork shimmers

blue as the day the artist first froze
those waves. Patience, Charlie says –
she has more of it than most!
Like the rowing boat

almost but not eternally
at the shingle, and like the Gulls
almost but not eternally in the sky,
and like the wind whipping rocks to sand

Eva will soon complete her work.
Final orders will be called:
Charlie will carry pork belly
and steaming apple pie

back to his council flat on the Lonnen
and we'll all lie in bed
listening for the crunch of keel
on pebble at the moonlit shore.

from **Sketchbook**

after drawings by George McVay and poems by James
Kirkup, collected in *Shields Sketches*

'This is a world with no horizon, excepting | Where we
stand together.' – James Kirkup, 'The End of the World'

1.   South Pier, Tynemouth

Since we must begin somewhere
let it be in this whirlpool:
where the sky's foundation
is the ceiling of the ocean
and miscible storm clouds
send the weathervane into waltz.

Your ghost glides unbroken
by the boardwalk,
beneath the railings and down
seaweed-strewn steps
where you gave yourself
balls-first to the phosphorescence
and breathed for the first time
with the water.

2.   Ingham Infirmary

They knew it as a place for convalescence
in a town howked by graft:
an explosion at the chemical works,
the light aircraft smashed through the roof,
limbs lost to Westoe firedamp.

A blind masseur played the accordion
of your rib-cage, staunching

emphysema from your beaten lungs,
which on your worst days
you feared would collapse
as sycamores sagging in November.

Now they're shifting out neonatal.
What once was a sand-dance
is the bottle-neck of an egg-timer.

I guess it's true when they say
be careful what you wish for
that your wish could end up being
the town's snuffed candle.

3.   St. Hilda's

They hung a boat above the nave
to remind the congregation
of all the lives saved
not by going down on their honkers
at the altar, but by crafting timber,
making it buoyant, taking
to the spray no matter what
time the bell-tower clock
was frozen at.

You had hoped he'd stiffened
the hands at that time
to make them chime
with stanzas of your own.

Do not be foolish enough to think
that a stopped clock is a synecdoche
for man's lack of wisdom;
it only proves that we're in an era
past caring about the hour.

4.   Harton, St. Peter's

An exoskeleton of trees
do little to save the pedestrian,
head-first in a sinister gale,
blowing her brolly into a bowl
she'll later use to beg with.

Best to remember it rainy this way;
to not consider how ventricles slog on
despite the rest of the body's
desire to pack it all in.

5.   Thirty-six Views of Cleadon Hills
      (Condensed; superimposed)

Like Hokusai or Matisse
I am trying to create relief
in a series which might speak
to the whole I know
no longer exists.

6.   Herd Groyne Lighthouse, South Shields

Since we can't assume an ending
(or an ending that we'd like)
let's imagine this diorama
on an alien night.

Marsden Grotto is underwater:
beach-combers and donkeys
have become Ammonites.

Ocean Road is a river:
Lawe an island
unto itself.

You want it weirder?

Then stand at Clifford's Fort
and pray for an inverted mirage:
a hazy tease flickering
the point where the sea's
supposed to cede to the Tyne,
but where now you wouldn't dare
place your faith in standing firm.

From bow or bridge
of tug or tanker
the prospect of the coast
is an unfinished painting.

This easel he set
these words you wrote
the debt I owe both.

The horizon is little more
than etching on white:
a place we can sail beyond
in ferry-boats or poems.

The sun on scales
pushing the moon back down.

A189 Hymn

Suppose we're driving out to Newbiggin-by-the-Sea
spying on the couple solemn on that plinth.
Meadow pipits hover over redemptive waves
snarling an old pit town's song: where all the broken bottles
cemented into walls behind the Iona Club collage
carlin peas and gospels from Woodhorn's diamond days.
Or there's a northwesterly cleansing the Cheviots
and the Wansbeck shimmers like tinfoil in spring air
that fooled us into thinking we had it so good.
Bindweed gleams in the central reservation
and all along the verge from Cambois to Seaton Sluice
we send down the windows drawing lungfulls
of the afternoon's coconut staves.
How sweet-smelling the gorse, how little to be saved.

Cull

After Louisa Hodgson's painting, *The Collingwood Monument, Tynemouth, Trafalgar Night*

No-one ever plotted a course for the horizon
expecting to come back changed, yet no-one
who came back changed could explain how.

Despite claims to three generations in the grave
some doors always remain bolted.
Not all men dream of being cast as monuments.

Many more would assemble the bonfire –
snadging smoke in tendrils from the beach
giving form and relief to the dazzle-show.

All are complicit in the pageant, this story
of conquest by marionettes willing wood to stone
stone to bronze, bronze to gold, gold to glory.

Those who see how rays always stray
out from the prism understand the deception.
Repatriate the obelisks; raze these bastard shibboleths.

A Museum Closes in the North

'The more civilised the civilised/ the more barbarian the barbarians' —Anne Stevenson, 'Jarrow'

Soon an insolvency firm will arrive
with clip boards and check-boxes,
begin listing assets. Next door
to the gallery whose worlds
will not be viewed by those with jobs
to do, tapestries by Geordie
ex-blasters on part-time craft courses
will peel to the floor like the memory
of Palmer's and Red Ellen.
Pigs and chickens gone, the farm
out back will be measured to straw
and sinew. The market value of pork
timesed by square hectares of site.
A fortnight ago, when we hung
the exhibition, took spirit levels
and pencils, hammer and nail,
we did so thinking of our selves.
Now, as our poems and paintings
become potential resources
to shore against liquidation,
we think of the school trips,
the broke and the breaking.
Because if a museum isn't just
a repository; if it means more
than a funnel we attach
to people's heads
expecting history to go in,
coins to come out,
then let the North rise
and hear it sing before another part
of our past fades to a phantom limb.

Dawn Chorus: Cleadon Village

Think of it beginning as a crack
        beneath a door:
early titular thoughts
          the sky has
on its axis
          back towards us.

Somewhere in the smudge
          beyond high-rises
          and docks of the city
it gathers momentum
          much like a storm
          whose palms
          caress energy
from each node and fissure
          of this brittle earth.

          All the birds
we didn't have names for
in that flat above the roundabout
          have found their way
          to this sweet parenthesis
within smelling distance of the sea.

So listen as blackbirds and skylarks
          make eaves in The Cottage
          serenade the turnpike, Tilesheds,
each burrowing heart.

Something in the chatter
          of this avian crowd
matches the muscle
          in your ribcage

and the cornet
        of your Cochlea
strumming a song
        for the simple thrill
of its catch and resonance.

Boldon West Junction

Saint George's Cross
weeps from windows
at the back of Brockley Whins
where Buddleia and trampoline
springs back on to ballast
beside the slope down
to Boldon Burn whose mules
for years have tread clocks
of mud above the teeming Don.

For a second beyond
my *Guardian* and Metro
window I see a kid squeeze
through a gap in the fence
and it's bad but I imagine
his homemade bong,
tack, cowies and whizz.

At the church hall last month
Whinny spoke about the lack
of demand for one-pound
breakfasts: sliced white
and bacon unclaimed
by kids climbing garages
behind Saint John the Baptist
as I did at fourteen
only to see the view
from the top

not stay there.
And why would you
when anti-vandal paint
is a badge not a blotch
and you can be out

at Newton Garth farm
in five minutes torching
fields with the catch
of burnt barley
at your throat
knowing you did that,
you did that?

Boy

Boy, I confess, I was scared. Not of you, five-years-old, wearing a Spider-Man onesie, but of the boy they said you'd become. Boy, at seven you're swearing; at nine nicking Mars bars; ten dealing tabs on the school yard. TWOCd your first car at thirteen. Fifteen sees your second stint in young offenders. God help little men like me when you shed your boy-skin, boy. Had on. Your parents are pulling you close to pass even though I'm only here contemplating Crack Willows: how they weave in the wind making the kind of poetry Bede aspired to. Making the kind of poetry I want to believe Bede aspired to. Boy, they drew your string close, hurried past, while I wondered how much space there could be between us.

Sea Rocket

5,000 miles in a 747
have taken you to Harris Beach, Oregon,
to find Sea Rocket by the boardwalk
where nobody will ever know your name
and the place you've come from:

Seaburn, where the same genus of plant
stowed perchance in cargo holds
to unfurl in spores at Hendon Docks
now protrudes from dunes by the North Sea
which you know doesn't know your name.

Later, looking into the window front
of the Brookings branch of the Democrats
you're mistaken for an eager voter
who shares a common belief
in free access to public health care.

Pineapple Weed grows in the slats
of paving here, too – the way it does
on the Ash path where your parents live.
Some things you know the names for,
others you're yet to learn.

Roker Dolomite

Nil Desperandum Auspice Deo

When I heard that the two of you
had started driving out to churches
that autumn they first flooded
your veins with chemotherapy drugs
          I wasn't surprised
that the Roker Dolomite of St. Peter's
Upper Permian Magnesium Limestones
were some sort of solace.

Nor   as you poured tea
from an always-leaky pot
where once Ceolfrith blessed heads
and Cuthbert   and Aidan
called to the skies   was I surprised
to think of you taking comfort
in walls that had survived many storms.

And just as the scanners at the RVI
consecrate flesh and tissue for remission

petrologists' laser models of sacred buildings
reveal similar findings:

that half-buried   masonry
like half-burned   cells   remain
because people with cracked bodies
like churches with cracked roofs
say we will not be defeated
          we will not be defeated.

Riddles of Spuggy

'Britain, formerly known as Albion, is an island in the ocean, lying towards the north west at a considerable distance from the coasts of Germany, Gaul and Spain, which together form the greater part of Europe...' —Bede, *The Ecclesiastical History of the English People*, Chapter 1: 'The situation of Britain and Ireland: their earliest inhabitants', 731

I.

Between twin monasteries I cracked from egg,
on bow-branch beyond the slake
in nest-bed within the sacred walls.
Witness to wax tablet and plainsong;
every processional below the belfry
under whose candlelight history was made.

II.

And Benedict did set out a decree
to build in the after-image of Rome
a house of sanctity out above the river bank
where waters whip cliffs to sand
and a hard northern gale blows;
and in it ye shall set down and try to answer
all the questions the Lord shall ask of ye.

III.

My mission is a simple one:
I'm a collector of stories and old songs;
a witness to the tale. Elegant plumage.

Your quest, my friend, furrowed as you are,
may be more difficult to discern.

IV.

Bequeathed a task by the highest power,
you've been asked to go out and record the world:
tell of the angle of sunlight cast onto wave,
speak of the silent way neap-tide crests.
And don't forget to align what's down here
with what's up there: the star-source
from where we've all come and where surely
our earthly bodies will vanish to.

V.

And later Benedict did rule that a second house
on the south shores of the Tyne
would make two monasteries linked as one,
and from there scribes would venture to measure
the horizon and refract light in the Mediterranean style.
Whether traversed by ground or skulked
by coble, the two places would conjoin,
mile-markers and ash-paths collapsed so that
when the ways were set down in codex,
stored in scriptorium, a tale would emerge:
sent from the North out to the World.

from **A String of Bedes**

716

Watches Ceolfrith kiss the heads of priests
and crying abbots before plodging into the Wear.
Shouts, 'wait!' and hands him the *Codex Amiatinus*
which he forgot. Waves him off over to Hendon, Hull,
then Rome, to live a higher life with St. Paul.

2005

Witnesses the Volkswagen Golf
spinning off Moor Lane narrowly avoiding
crushing me and Matt on our way to Whitburn New Fields
to play football with the lads. Takes the tab
from the hand of the drunk driver, who in years to come
will swear he sparked up in the crumpled chassis.

1771

Cradles the babby washed up at South Shields
after drifting down the swollen Tyne
from the ruined Roman bridge in the autumn surge.
Rumours that babby clung to a copy of the *Ecclesiastical
    History*
washed clean from Charnley's bookshop, unconfirmed.

2003

Fails to hide a smirk and chortles uncontrollably
as I cinematically wrap my arm around VH and tell her
we'll be 'foh-eva' one summer dusk evening at Cleadon mill.

1977

Is there for Muhammad Ali's visit to Gypsy's Green,
in the red corner for his spar with Reg Long.
Later, orders a Greggs cheese pasty on Frederick Street
and watches from the top of the mosque as thousands
    gather
for the marriage blessing of the 'Louisiana Lip'.

2010

Chases down the Vauxhall Astra containing the lads
who set about me and my mates one snowy Christmas
at Westoe Village. Their punishment: reciting the virtues
of good, Christian morals to schoolchildren in Hedworth.

1930

Attempts to calm both police and Yemeni rioters
at Mill Dam with passages from the *Voyage of St Brendan*.
Spends the evening in Holborn and High Shields
in solidarity with the sailors.

1996

Incants passages from *Eddius Stephanus: Life of Wilfrid* –
'The bishop prayed after the manner of Elias and Eliseus
and gave his blessing. The breath of life returned to the
    boy.' –
to revive my Dad's cruciate knee ligament enough
to get him out of Roker Park after over-enthusiastically
celebrating a conciliatory goal in a 2–1 loss to Wolves.

1985

Ignores Barry MacSweeney's calls via the ham radio.
Leaves him to eat seaweed at Druridge Bay
and think about what he's done.

2019

Is external examiner for my PhD viva at Newcastle
    University.
Passes me with minor corrections.
We celebrate in the Hotspur bar with mead and scampi fries.

1855

Plays parlour games with Margaret Wilcox and Charles
    Dodgson
overlooking Whitburn Steel. Tells C about the time
he saw a walrus beached at Marsden and the best
    techniques
for fashioning a watertight coracle from local willow.

1999

Snow falls hard on the trestle table bar
as he helps wor kid make Skol ice lollies.
Uncle Mal rolls his ankle on the icy patio and is helped
to the settee by the hands of a saint
and my Dad's best mates.
As the clock ticks twelve over Harton,
fireworks go up like a Benediction

1832

Rows across Jarra Slake – Jarrow's Lake – to Jobbling
gibbeted like a turkey. Tar, feathers.
Knows nothing good can come of attempted rescue
but sits anyway beneath the caged bird
as slowly its heart beats out to the blackened Tyne.

Lambton Drops

They appear as spectres
on paved-over wagon ways
from Seaham Harbour
to Ryhope Colliery:

Phantasmic Mackems
fingers like rivets
chatting of Austin and Pickersgill's.

How they suddenly emerge
from chares and lonnens
at the back of Dragonville
or the gravity track

from Warden Law –
their compass always bent
back, their Scotty dogs loyal –

like they've burst the frame
of a Norman Cornish
only to squeeze
into Lowry's image of Lambton Drops.

I know they hanker
the naptha-stained riverbanks
of those *simpler times*
in the way that I too have dreamed
of a *job for life*.

Or maybe it's not the mercury
plummeting below zero
in a dry-dock on the Wear

but their bait boxes
and communion cards
these diaphanous sods crave.

The funeral cortège
stopping one last time
at the Mill View Social
on its way to Saint Hild and Bedes.

Post-Psychogeographic

Not another peregrination
by a white man
in all the kit
following a minor river
in northern England
likening its course
to the pulse of the nation.

Not another pilgrimage
by a man of dubious faith
stuffed on cereal bars
tracing Anglo-Saxon
ambiance onto a bridleway
flanked by pesticides and polymers
of uncertain origin.

Not another proselytiser
of a defunct *genius loci*
copying binomial nomenclature
from an Amazon-bought
book of wildflowers
hoping to assuage the lack
of a sub-regional topography.

Not another polemic
by a poet stuck for synonyms;
stuck, indeed, for much
meaningful to say about the minor
river, its muddled
communities not ~~seeking~~
~~documentation~~ arsed.

Each Pebble Its Part

Not my North

North   My North

Every word I put down
every line break
stanza, sequence – not enough

Basil, your Northern landscapes
are not my Northern landscapes

I'm here at Marsden Bay
with two elderly dogs
the only girl I've ever thought to marry
two hundred miles away

You are dead and you cannot help me

I write of the swift flight of spuggy
thinking – as you didn't – of Bede

How do I live in a place
whose sparrows
are in terminal decline?

Some days it is easier to remember
than to live

I have amputated
myself into
a life
I partially inhabit.

As for love –
sometimes a cwtch means more
    than hiraeth or hyem

        Basil, your Northern landscapes
                    are not my Northern landscapes

And these days we drown in the bogus

        Wired up in ways
you'd barely comprehend
        making notes in your Moleskin
on the train to Wylam

If there is such thing as a 'poet's vision'
    then let me seize it—
        Hoy this phone, this laptop into the Tyne
            and I will not decline
                to walk, to log, to legislate
                    my true North, true Love
                        truly gan hyem

My North   North   Not my North

        My brother and sister say they'd never come
        back
if none of our family lived here

        We are one marriage or job away from exile

                    I have thought
                to pick up each pebble
            on Shields beach

What would it mean to lose the sand
    strip away each grain?
                I have thought about my mates
              pulled by the sodium glare
      of middle English towns
    so far from the smell of the sea

Pulled like iron filings
    to the magnetic thrust
        of The City

              I have thought
What would it mean

      At slack tide
    Your poem burns too bright.
     How should I write?

      Each

Pebble   its

     Part.

Pons Aelius City Limits

Adept in syntaxes of stronghold,
synonyms for self-interest, we understand
solid geometries of the portcullis:
you have your side, we have ours.

One plane of the gated barbican
might have invited praise for oaks felled,
riveted to steel; the other for weaponry
several centuries off.

But how ridiculous these macka walls,
like Creatined arms of Glaswegian stags
who one hour earlier passed
on a Virgin Pendolino over Forth Street

and are now in the Victoria Comet
chugging vodka Red Bulls, look to those
of us who've seen the city at peace.
But then, why leave vestigial fortresses

other than to honour the gore-stotted
chares from where our ancestors
flung, or else were clarted in, pitch and tar
and where some still are sticklers for blood?

Imagining the diorama escalated:
Castle Garth pounding with flame,
Side engulfed, some subtle twists in history's
Rubik's Cube aligned differently

and I might feel the urgency of this place.
As-is, I'm simply ten miles ago, twenty years
away, another black gate marking
boundaries of my bairnhood play

on Armstrong Avenue, South Shields,
where a German Shepherd with a Himmler-
esque name bore fang and snarl
the way its ancestors were bred to:

manifesting a scene in which we devise schemes
to mark and guard colonies whose conquest
and record by bayonet-blow, land registry,
longship or Royal Charter

nearly always fade to points
of abstraction beyond which it becomes
impossible to tell where sprung blood
became curdled ink.

Murmurations

Termini, dusk, Starlings over Piazza del Cinquecento
inviting implausible metaphors from those
prone to staring into rivers: Tiber and Tyne flowing on.
Taxi drivers complain of bird-brine while all eyes
of the Romantically-inclined are drawn
to the apotheosis offered by a fractal of feathers –
how our dance here defines the manner of our leaving.

On Not Finding Bede

At the throat of the Don
  where twin Tyne tunnels
undercut Crackwillow
  we searched for you.

We searched for you
  in Go-To-Bed-At-Noons,
by Pellitory-Of-The-Wall,
  through Lady's Bedstraw.

At Station Burn, Field Scabious
  could have been your glow;
Black Medic your remedy.
  We searched for you

the way Small Tortoiseshells
  and Meadow Browns
search Timothy and Tansy;
  how miners' caged Linnets

trace Bernician sky.
  We thought we traced
your coracle over Whitburn Steel;
  clouds scattering

for your arrival, but as we looked
  beyond Souter Point
we could only see waves –
like praying hands of saints.

Grapnel

The summer the Belgian carriers
fixed themselves off Tynemouth
my uncle would invite me down the beach
for paper cups of coffee from Minchella's
and we'd sit on the decorative new benches
paid for with E.U. cash and squint
at the horizon: past my cousins
and the dogs jumping rolling waves
to where a mile or two off the coast
they'd thrown down grapnel.
And though I knew we weren't there
to look at or talk about those ships
I could tell by the way he clasped the cup
how much he really needed a fag
that I should focus on the sea
not mention politics or family
or the politics of families
so that as long as nothing was said
we could concentrate solely
the way men do
on the scrunch of sand
between his children's toes
or the dogs' animal instinct to nose
seaweed air and while there was still
dregs in our cups could consider
barnacles climbing up chains of anchor
and what it might mean to hanker
adrift and how long you should wait
before sending up the flare.

The Campaign Team for a Federal Northumbria is Stuck on King Edward VII Bridge

When they left platform zero and the terminus
of the beast behind, this is not what they foresaw
pining for the first vistas of Spartan territory:
wrought iron bridges spanning the river
like a homely welcome: *Hiya, hinny*; *Alreet, mate?*

But as the sky Gods of Tyne seem intent
on keeping them suspended above Skinnerburn Road
in an ever-warming vestibule for the next hour at least,
let them push away thoughts of the crees at Low Fell,
god-honest folk bread-lining the border.

Hydro-spirits of the tidal estuary, they will secede
to any of your demands for five more minutes
on the platform. Some are even going so far
as to consider abandoning the whole bloody project
in exchange for just one lung-full of unrecycled air!

And if the ghost of Stephenson did appear to shudder
at the thought of what his steam machine has become,
then let that not concern the magnanimous denizens
of coach B, beholden to pie charts and projections
of what a *Haliwerfolc* confederacy could be.

For Saint Nick and James, Saint Cookson, too
are reflected in the slick of these riverbank currents;
this flight path of the kittiwakes beneath Redheugh,
where the sun dropping behind Whickham
lights the static carriages stuck on the bridge

in a golden penumbra which, if only they would
take the time to look, might have them all moved.

M56 Hymn

Just for today, let me stand on this forecourt
nozzle in hand pumping testosterone
and ancient sun-light and not feel a millilitre
of shame for my gender or carbon footprint.

Let me sit in the inside lane of the M56
sun sinking in the rear-view over Moel Famau
like a hard-boiled egg, pilot lights
on chemical sites at Little Stanney and Runcorn

pulsing as retro arcade games. Let the man
on the radio telling it the way he wants it to be
for the dawn of a new America not concern me.
Leave platitude and sentiment to rot online

and instead bid me shift up to sixth; the thrust
of a German TDI beneath my right foot and arse
the only thrill today demands. Allow me to shrug
off my default masculinity, bringing you into

this poem, but not as a caricature or device.
Pray it not come across as trite when I say
that I want today following signs for THE NORTH
to amount to nothing more than our hands holding

across the handbrake. For the issues beyond
tires and tarmac needn't be worthy of further
exposition, when we've a full tank, grab bag of crisps
and the road and night ahead are long.

Wannabe

The second time I was kicked in the balls
I was punched in the face.
A glancing palm
in the school yard before form:
Gaz C's boxing moves gone wrong
or right.
        That night I thought of nothing
        but the bull's-eye of his crown;
        my own fist coming down.

*

The third time I was kicked in the balls
I was twenty-three and pissed.
Outside The County pub in Shields,
some lads set about us.
I still wade through red mist.

*

The last time I was kicked in the balls
there was no physical violence.
The 23rd June 2016 was the day
the glacier cracked
              and there's not much more
              I can say about that

so let's go back to the first time
I was kicked in the balls:

Summer, '96, Monkton Stadium.
A half-volley ricocheted
from the foot of a boy three years my senior.

I'm down on the Astro,
other lads crowding 'round,
some singing 'Wannabe' by the Spice Girls.

I see my mother in a halo of stars
                    Oh, son, it hurts less the second time

Self-Portrait in Passport Photobooth

Enter the confessional: rectangular space
where your face bounced back
asks how compliant you've been, how vain.
When you're ready, press to begin.
Forgive me, Lord, for I have ignored
Spice-ruined lives and holes in the net.
Maybe the net, by its very design, requires

holes. Are these thoughts sly or shrewd?
asks my face, five times: thumbnails of my ego
in three-day stubble, neutral expression,
no glasses. If I draw a plastic curtain,
adjust chair, adjust hair, slot pound-coins,
might I become official? A face like mine
requires few modifications: simply wipe

the screen, align my eyes. Ready?
There is no way I can resist the second
and third attempt. Nothing wrong
with the first snap, I am simply basking
in the cocoon the booth forms 'round me;
passing commuters perhaps glancing
my shoes, lower legs, leather satchel.

Passing without thought to pause.
Shoals of people at Old Eldon Square
push prams, Jehovah's Kingdom,
broadband deals, sausage and bean melts.
With an official thumb, I push OK.
Close the curtain, pretend not to pray.
Slight adjustment, stamped, ready.

Thirty seconds for the photos to steady.
My face five times in my palm reminds
that not all is spirit, some still is carbon.
This is entirely me, raw in three-day
stubble, neutral expression, no glasses.
I have stared into the light and crossed
beyond, hoping always to blend right in.

Buddleia davidii: Tyne↔Mersey

From this tunnel below Trinity Square
where I've been birthed before
I emerge to a view
of Liverpool's twin cathedrals.

I have forgotten the religions
they preach and which way round
but that's sound

as I swear I was just staring
at the spire of Saint Nick's
and the Byker Wall.

Now I'm zooming through Tranmere
and Port Sunlight
carrying a bit of Felling
and Pelaw with me.

Now I'm zooming through Felling
and Pelaw
carrying a bit of Tranmere
and Port Sunlight with me.

Flower of the railways
sprouting along tracks from Gateshead
to Birkenhead. Two hundred years back
blown only by Sichuan breeze.

Weed in one language
flower in another.

Correct your apps: Newcastle is not Manhattan!

Shopkeepers on East 34th in Murray Hill
shovelling snow into clumps
ploughs will later churn up
remind me of men digging coal
which is outlandish
as I've never witnessed it
but I'm led to believe
it happened like this

For a while we were covered in the stuff
it changed everything
then the weather turned
melting as if it had never snowed at all

Davy

I took Great-Granda Nick's Davy lamp
down to the tool shed, set it on the chest freezer,
glugged paraffin into the base,
sparked the flue and waited for ignition.

Hoping to enter his life and times,
to return and hold them as models,
I'd imagined the bowels beneath Boldon
and Westoe: firedamp sky of worlds

more rich despite their autarky.
I have heard that the absence of flames
makes the shivering castaway pine more
cruelly, sends him hallucinating

snakes of naptha and kerosene.
All along he knew the slag-heaps and wagon
chares, the weight of the earth above
and the distances still to go.

Ornamental now, Davy's become a puzzle
and Nicholas is muzzled.
Get out of this sink estate, Nick:
buff your boots, recite the Lord's prayer,

slick back your hair and hold your chest high.
You're out of the shaft now, air is crisp.
Put the lamp on the mantle and inhale.
Breathe without thinking of breathing.

A483 Hymn

I am working my way through gristly names
of communities rising above Oxeye Daisy
and tab packets strewn along the hard shoulder
where Iffor Williams trailers rustle sheep
and class-C drugs into and out of Denbigshire.

483 carry us – for twenty more miles
to a place twinned with *hyem*.

A gargle of consonants:
Rhosllanerchrugog, Llay, Cefn-Mawr.

Past the Bersham slag heap
doing 75 in the outside lane,
Robert Saint's Hebburn connects
with Clwyd and the miners' hymn
via my machinations on the lingua-
franca of toil and sweat.

Your parents remember the days before the bypass,
where now you can get a Chicken Madras
from a roadside caff, take it back to a static caravan
on cud-land overlooking the Ceiriog Valley.

Half-remembered *Mabinogi* tales rise
with the damp and daffodils nodding
by the steam railway speak of a *hiraeth*
that can be engraved onto slate coasters
or painted on a travel mug.

Little of that for us, when a talking head
on Radio Two suggests we're entering a new Cold War.
When I think of the future I think of the causeway
at Lindisfarne: those who chance it despite the warnings.

Known and unknown variables, I'll do what I can
for now: shift down through the gears,
flick the indicator and follow signs
for Ifton Heath to park up
in the porch of my step-country.

Toll

In the cab which I've hailed from some realm
      between the precious metals
      microelectromechanical accelerometer
      and microprocessing units
on my palm and a Catherine Wheel of satellites above us
      I rummage in my jeans for shrapnel
as the driver and I both realise that the toll
      needs to be paid.
          When handing over
      coins warmed by my thighs
it's not just the barrier we see rise
         but some partition between us:
all these tolls through which our lives unfold
      and the alchemy made in their crossing.

Blood Test

Past the dashboard, bonnet, limit of the car park,
past Cow Parsley in clumps footing the field.
Past logs loaded on lorries paused on another
minor road halted by temporary traffic lights.

Past Kronospan spuming steam becoming clouds
rising over hills rising precisely as you'd expect
in a North Wales town: the type we might one day
winch our guy-ropes to, which brings me back

to you in the hospital behind, the tourniquet
tightened, the needle going in, a bruise
the shade of the sky if it was eight hours later
blossoming on your arm and back in the car

my thoughts on all of this beginning to roam
precisely as you'd expect them to were I at home.

The Last Home Match of the Year

After, and with apologies to, Paul Farley.
R.I.P. Bradley Lowery.

The ref raises whistle to lips
as our goalie jogs to the centre-circle
hanging big palms round the shoulders
of our full-back and captain
        making a link
with the linesmen, fourth official,
visiting team and fans
whose marras once did the same
in clotted coal shafts beneath.

We're duly asked over the Tannoy
to observe a moment's silence
for the players, supporters and club representatives
who've passed this year.

As the whistle blasts,
sucking all attention to the sky
(ideal blue as the day Pangaea
first cracked or when MacGregor was pushed
to the cold ground at Ellington),
forty-thousand people cross their hands,
tune to the backing fuzz of floodlights,
that one lonely Seagull's cry.

Electric advertising hoardings flash to no-one
in this moment which is strictly carbon and chlorophyll.
Looking from the patch of atmosphere
the stadium frames back to the touch-line
we envisage rings drawing closer:
who'll be left next year to sing the lads in?

Part of us wants this moment
arm-to-arm with parents, grandparents, pals
to last past dusk, through next week, eclipsing
Christmas and the shambles we've witnessed.
But already some bloke in his lucky, striped scarf
three pints in, odds looking good
is itching in the south stand as the ref
once again raises whistle to lips
to bellow *Haway*! bring the life back in
and send the year on its way.

A Hungarian Courier Watches South Shields Vs Ryton & Crawcrook Albion

'Everything belongs by right to those who care for it'—Bertolt Brecht, *The Caucasian Chalk Circle*

Nar, he didn't croon like a jackal
beneath a honeypot moon
nor scoff a saveloy dip on Wembley Way
but he did watch minutes croak doon
eight months earlier on top of his lorry
as fork-lift truck drivers by-day
chased down weeknight wingers.
So save some silver for the sojourner
who set up his tabernacle for the night,
the lot of w' joined beneath the floodlights.

Dispatches from the Troll Factory

'The starting point of critical elaboration is the
consciousness of what one really is, and is 'knowing
thyself' as a product of the historical processes to date
which has deposited in you an infinity of traces, without
leaving an inventory. The first thing to do is to make such
an inventory.' —Antonio Gramsci, *Selections from the
Prison Notebooks of Antonio Gramsci*

At the u-bend of a northern town,
on an industrial estate by a builders' merchants,
there's a non-descript, windowless silo
shut off to the smell of boiling saveloys
where a troll factory is on overtime.

Once, they pressed Navy biscuits here,
sprayed blood from carcasses,
panned salt, welded ships, forged steel.
Now, fingers fire across keys mimicking
caulking, riveting, shovel and pick.
Manufactured assent.

Riveting stories are being written
by a team of lackies on zero-hours contracts.
Un-unionised labour, they beg
for thirty seconds extra to wipe their arses,
for the thermostat to be knocked down.

Here's the listicle
What the EU has done for Britain
counterposed with
News from Nissan: Sewing Seeds on the Shop Floor.

Here's the fabricated op-ed by a Labour MP,
chinks in its armour already Tommy-Gunned
by Windows warriors.

Its riposte – True Blue Tory dogma
by a former chancellor of the exchequer –
will be launched next week, ready to be torched
by an eager set of caps-locked claws.
Red in tooth and poor.

They're knocking out fake profiles by the minute:
frothing NIMBYs, centrist dads,
the avocado and flat white brigade.
Non-binary acronyms yet to enter discourse
but sure to be politely queried
by a PPE graduate with the latest solidarity
slogan pinned to his thumbnail.

Theirs is the Scorched Earth theory
of deregulated journalism.
Comments are launched, buoyed, shelled,
life-vested, rifled, flamethrown, defenestrated,
patched back up, kicked, cackled,
heckled, praised, jeered, leered, seered
or otherwise dissolved in tinnitus and apraxia.

Headlines meet counter-headlines
meet sub-tweets meet top comments (unfiltered):

    Full luxury Communism...WHENEVER!

    Smash the Nanny State: How You Can Help

    Feast from the East: Muslims Feed City Homeless

    ECLUSIVE: Putin meddles in Mars Mission

Like servers processing cryptocurrency
in the prairies of Alberta,
the exothermic heat generated by their work
could be its undoing.

Here all the clickbait and pop-ups,
all the roulette ads and financial promises
from kings of small African nations
will meld with (or sink) the sanctimonious
and heartfelt alike.

Bless recently-retired Deidre,
66 from County Down, who only wanted
to check in with friends from Bridge on Facebook.

Commiserations to Jim, 57, from Jarrow
who only bought a smartphone
to get the latest odds on the game
and express his discontent at bureaucrats.

Deidre and Jim are bits in a programme
no-one remembers writing.

Theirs are the bull horn paintings marked in caves
at Lascaux: the outlined palms we took
to mean *Hello*, when what they meant was *Stop*.

At the u-bend of a northern town,
a smell not dissimilar to boiling saveloys
begins to waft: the blockage is gathering heft.

Harton Rise

Everything smells of the ocean floor
and Catholicism at North Shields fish quay
where I'm waiting with my grandparents
for haddock, chips and peas.

Across the seas, old battle axes sharpen,
but back in their garden
Asters are coming into bloom,
tomatoes bulging to ripeness.

Behind, the cemetery is nearly full
but they've picked out their patch:
a corner grave adjacent to the church
from where they'll plot star-trails.

In the soil below, bottles from the Victorian tip
still capped with silicosis.
The same earth nourishes the apple tree.
Swifts are darting through it.

Shield | Yield

Aa want nowt more to dee with it | 'til the tide gans oot.

—

Ease with which the gradient of the beach falters, the
 current's sneck catches.

—

Before you've had time to chew your pulse
you're out above the nipples
legs flicking as ballerinas.

—

Swim between the flags
say signs on the foreshore.

—

First place-name learned
        when armour, defence, screen and ward
        had no definition and home meant
        counting a skimming pebble's nod.

                                        Shield.

—

Then home meant:
  wanting to be the pebble; imagining the horizon as
  handle to grip; magnetic thrust of waves; beauty of blue
  and its prospect; iron-bar certainty of ambit.

                                        Yield.

—

Then home meant:
        anchoring to ripples.

—

Coast withering as reversed origami.

—

(At the point of asphyxiation or hypothermia the body
  appears hyperactive.)

—

Swim between the flags.

—

Rampart, guard, bulwark, shelter.
Anchored to a ripple.

—

—between the—

—

Then home meant:
   Looking for the pebble falling in slow-motion beneath the
   waves: its gathering density marked by lichen bedding
   down in the erratic.

—

Then home meant:
   Finding another home, which felt like adultery: intense –
   pronged with lemon and sugar – it was understood to be the
   only way when pebble had been beseeched by tide,
   smoothed to nothing by undercurrents and ecology's ripples.

—

Counting a skimming pebble's nod.

—

I want nothing more to do with it | 'til the tide comes back.

A184 Hyem

for Kate, rarely wrong

Gods of Askew Road
Gods of Fulwell Quarry

Help us find voice
or bid us be hushed.

Let wheat fields flicker
see Poppies glow.

Whether eastbound
westbound or a destination
we don't yet know

pray see to it
that we get there together.

Landing at Ponteland International

Don't jolt me awake
with a descent in altitude,
a fasten seatbelt sign,
the captain coming over the intercom.
            My mind is somewhere on the continent
            lagging behind my cranium,
            pressed to the plastic shield on the window.

Don't make me make patterns
of this abstract sequence of orange lights:
I don't want to know where I am tonight.

            The coast will arrive
            as an absence of illumination
            and before I've had chance to say
            arrivederci   or   alreet

            I'll be counting lighthouses,
            estates with known drug problems
            then every potboiler the province has subsumed

      so at the last second, as if caught in a gale
      let the trip resume—

—have us pull up hard, hard back up.
We're in the movies now,
the journey entirely fanciful.
            So hit the throttle, race the sun.
            Put time-zones between
            the problem, solve it later on.

Make me plead that we circle
Ponteland for as long as there's fuel
left in the tanks.

All the fields and railways and fables
below appear pliant from above.

But just because I can hold the whole
of this vista between forefinger and thumb

doesn't mean I've got the measure of it.

Songline: Cleadon Hills

Since spuggies no longer sing and the wind has locked around you,
since satellites fell from the firmament setting the needle in spin.
Since scorched turf in the shadow of the disused reservoir
doesn't speak of much beyond chemical compounds and
   combustion,
because flames leeching from bonnets and indicator bulbs popping
under hallucinogenic heat are as banal up here as pissing into the
   sea,
let us praise instead something of the cylinders and pistons
within our deposed jockey: the one for whom a tea-towel-wrapped
   fist
thrown through the window frame is a temporary visa
to suburban fame – sodium streetlights lining the boulevard
from the Scotch Estate to Sunniside Lane applauding
their rally-track name as tarmac conks out and chambers go *boom*.
Before unleaded is troughed over the back seats, let us feel
as they did that night streams of prophetic light from an austere
   moon,
to stand above the town looking down like an overthrown Kaiser,
strike a match, take a bow and send the red curtain falling.

Jake Morris-Campbell was born in South Shields, Tyne and Wear, in 1988. He is the author of two pamphlets of poetry: *The Coast Will Wait Behind You* (Art Editions North, 2015) and *Definitions of Distance* (Red Squirrel Press, 2012).

In 2021 he was selected as a BBC/AHRC New Generation Thinker. His work has appeared on BBC Radio 3's *Free Thinking* and in magazines, newspapers and journals including *Ambit*, *Poetry London* and *The Rialto*. Jake holds a PhD in Creative Writing from Newcastle University, where he works part-time as a research and teaching assistant. A freelance writer, editor and tutor, he is also Visiting Lecturer in Creative Writing at the University of Chester. A winner of New Writing North's Andrew Waterhouse award, he regularly contributes to collaborative public arts projects. He lives in South Tyneside with his wife and children.

Corrigenda for Costafine Town is his first full collection.